Are You A Bully?

by Sam Williams

Content Consultant:
Melissa Z. Pierce, L.C.S.W.

Rourke
Educational Media

rourkeeducationalmedia.com

Teacher Notes available at
rem4teachers.com

www.rourkeeducationalmedia.com

Dedicated- To my parents and sisters –Sam

Melissa Z. Pierce is a licensed clinical social worker with a background in counseling in the home and school group settings. Melissa is currently a life coach. She brings her experience as a L.C.S.W. and parent to the *LIttle World Social Skills* collection and the *Social Skills and More* program.

PHOTO CREDITS: Cover: © Christopher Futcher; Page 3: © Steven Robertson; Page 5: © Craig Dingle; Page 7: © Mark Bowden; Page 9: © Ana Abejon; Page 11, 13: © monkeybusinessimages; Page 15: © Thomas Gordon; Page 17: © Karen Struthers; Page 19: © Chris Schmidt; Page 21: © IdeaBug Media
Illustrations by: Anita DuFalla

Edited by: Precious McKenzie

Cover and Interior designed by: Tara Raymo

Library of Congress PCN Data

Are You a Bully? / Sam Williams
(Little World Social Skills)
ISBN 978-1-61810-134-1 (hard cover)(alk. paper)
ISBN 978-1-61810-267-6 (soft cover)
Library of Congress Control Number: 2011945279

Rourke Educational Media
Printed in the United States of America,
North Mankato, Minnesota

rourkeeducationalmedia.com

customerservice@rourkeeducationalmedia.com   •   PO Box 643328 Vero Beach, Florida 32964

Bullies use words or actions to pick on people.

Some bullies call kids names they don't like.

How would you feel if you were called names?

Everyone likes to be **included** in the **group.**

Some bullies leave kids out of the group.

What can you do to make someone a part of the group?

Some bullies **threaten** to hit other kids.

Most kids are **scared** of bullies.

What should she do?

Some bullies steal another kid's lunch.

Some bullies take another kid's markers without asking.

Who should she talk to?

17

If you are being **bullied**, tell an **adult**.

What Would You Do...

If a classmate was calling you names every day?

If you saw someone else getting picked on?

If someone at school never let you play with the rest of the class?

Picture Glossary

adult (uh-DUHLT):
A fully grown person is called an adult.

bullied (BUL-eed):
To be picked on by another person.

group (groop):
A number of people that go together.

included (in-klood-id):
When someone is allowed to be a part of something.

scared (skaird):
When you feel frightened or afraid.

threaten (THRET-uhn):
When someone says that they will hurt you.

Index

adult   18

bullied   18

group   6, 8, 9

scared   12

threaten   10

Websites

www.kidsource.com

www.mrsp.com

www.speakaboos.com

About the Author

Sam Williams lives with his two dogs, Abby and Cooper, in Florida. Abby is sometimes a bully to Cooper. Cooper uses a strong bark to stand up to Abby when she is being mean.

Ask The Author!
www.rem4students.com